A TALE OF MONSTROUS EXTRAVAGANCE

A Tale of
MONSTROUS
Extravagance

IMAGINING
MULTILINGUALISM

HENRY KREISEL LECTURE SERIES

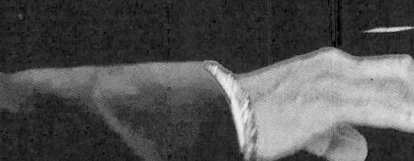

The University of Alberta Press

Tomson
HIGHWAY

Published by

The University of Alberta Press
Ring House 2
Edmonton, Alberta, Canada T6G 2E1
www.uap.ualberta.ca

and

Canadian Literature Centre / Centre de
littérature canadienne
3–5 Humanities Centre
University of Alberta
Edmonton, Alberta, Canada T6G 2E5
www.abclc.ca

Copyright © 2015 Tomson Highway
Introduction copyright © 2015 Christine
Sokaymoh Frederick

LIBRARY AND ARCHIVES CANADA
CATALOGUING IN PUBLICATION

Highway, Tomson, 1951–, author
    A tale of monstrous extravagance :
imagining multilingualism
/ Tomson Highway.

(Henry Kreisel memorial lecture series)
Issued in print and electronic formats.
ISBN 978-1-77212-041-7 (pbk.).—
ISBN 978-1-77212-071-4 (pdf).—
ISBN 978-1-77212-069-1 (epub).—
ISBN 978-1-77212-070-7 (kindle)

    1. Multilingualism and literature.
2. Language and culture. 3. Highway,
Tomson, 1951– –Anecdotes. I. Canadian
Literature Centre, issuing body II. Title.
III. Series: Henry Kreisel lecture series

PN171.M93H55 2015   809   C2014-908272-X
                            C2014-908273-8

First edition, first printing, 2015.
Printed and bound in Canada by Houghton
Boston Printers, Saskatoon, Saskatchewan.
Copyediting by Peter Midgley.
The Cree language feedback for the Highway
lecture was provided by Solomon Ratt of
First Nations University, William Dumas of
Manitoba First Nations Education Resource
Centre, and Arden Ogg of the Cree Literacy
Network.

The University of Alberta Press is committed
to protecting our natural environment.
As part of our efforts, this book is printed
on Enviro Paper: it contains 100% post-
consumer recycled fibres and is acid- and
chlorine-free.

The Canadian Literature Centre
acknowledges the support of the Alberta
Foundation for the Arts for the Henry
Kreisel Lecture delivered by Tomson
Highway in March 2014 at the University
of Alberta.

The University of Alberta Press gratefully
acknowledges the support received for
its publishing program from The Canada
Council for the Arts. The University of
Alberta Press also gratefully acknowledges
the financial support of the Government
of Canada through the Canada Book Fund
(CBF) and the Government of Alberta
through the Alberta Media Fund (AMF)
for its publishing activities.

Canada Canada Council Conseil des Arts
        for the Arts   du Canada

Alberta
Government

FOREWORD
The CLC Kreisel Lecture

*In this event we come together, listen with more than our
ears, remove blinders and become part of the celebration,
expand our thinking and feeling of inclusion, and build
relationships.*

—CHRISTINE SOKAYMOH FREDERICK[1]

THE FUNDAMENTAL OBJECTIVE of the Henry Kreisel
Memorial Lecture Series could not be better summarized.
This series realizes most fully the Canadian Literature
Centre's mission: to bring together authors, readers,
students, researchers and teachers in an open, inclusive
and critical forum. Kreisel lecturers already include Joseph
Boyden, Wayne Johnston, Dany Laferrière, Eden Robinson,
Annabel Lyon, Lawrence Hill, Esi Edugyan, and now the
awe-inspiring showman *par excellence*, Tomson Highway.
Take the fine points about social oppression, cultural
identities and sense of place by Boyden, or Johnston's
reflection on the tumultuous encounter of history and
fiction. Consider with Laferrière both the pains of exile

and the joys of migrancy, or the personal and communal ethics of Aboriginal storytelling that Robinson presents. Antiquity and the present come together through Lyon's lecture about the creative process of historical fiction. Hill invokes the need for an informed conversation about book censorship. And in these pages, Highway makes a compelling argument for the truly liberating, and joy-giving, aspects of knowing *other and others' languages,* including, if not foremost, the language of music.

The lectures in the Kreisel series confront questions that concern us all in the specificity of our contemporary experience, whatever our differences. In the spirit of free and honest dialogue, they do so with thoughtfulness and depth as well as with humour and elegance, all of which characterize, in one way or another, the eight incredibly talented writers featured so far.

These public lectures set out to honour Professor Henry Kreisel's legacy in an annual public forum. Author, University Professor and Officer of the Order of Canada, Henry Kreisel was born in Vienna into a Jewish family in 1922. He left his homeland for England in 1938 and was interned, in Canada, for eighteen months during the Second World War. After studying at the University of Toronto, he began teaching in 1947 at the University of Alberta, and served as Chair of English from 1961 until 1970. He served as Vice-President (Academic) from 1970 to 1975, and was named University Professor in 1975, the highest scholarly award bestowed on its faculty members by the University of Alberta. Professor Kreisel was an inspiring and beloved teacher who taught generations of students to love literature and was one of the first people to bring the experience of the immigrant to modern

Canadian literature. He died in Edmonton in 1991. His works include two novels, *The Rich Man* (1948) and *The Betrayal* (1964), and a collection of short stories, *The Almost Meeting* (1981). His internment diary, alongside critical essays on his writing, appears in *Another Country: Writings By and About Henry Kreisel* (1985).

The generosity of Professor Kreisel's teaching at the University of Alberta profoundly inspires the CLC in its public outreach, research pursuits, and continued commitment to the ever-growing richness and diversity of Canada's writings. The Centre embraces Henry Kreisel's no less than pioneering focus on the knowledge of one's own literatures. The CLC pursues a better understanding of a complicated and difficult world, which literature can reimagine and transform.

The Canadian Literature Centre was established in 2006, thanks to the leadership gift of the noted Edmontonian bibliophile, Dr. Eric Schloss.

MARIE CARRIÈRE
Director, Canadian Literature Centre
Edmonton, August 2014

NOTE
1. "Introduction," *A Tale of Monstrous Extravagance*, xiii.

LIMINAIRE
Les conférences Kreisel du CLC

> À l'occasion de cet événement, nous nous réunissons, nous
> écoutons avec plus que nos oreilles, nous retirons nos
> œillères et nous nous intégrons à la fête, nous enrichissons
> notre pensée et notre sentiment d'inclusion, et nous créons
> des relations.
>
> —CHRISTINE SOKAYMOH FREDERICK[1]

ON NE SAURAIT PAS MIEUX SYNTHÉTISER les objectifs
essentiels de la Série des Conférences Henry Kreisel.
Cette série réalise tout au mieux la mission du Centre de
littérature canadienne: celle de réunir auteurs, lecteurs,
étudiants, chercheurs et professeurs dans un forum
ouvert, inclusif et critique. Parmi les conférenciers de la
série Kreisel l'on peut déjà compter Joseph Boyden, Wayne
Johnston, Dany Laferrière, Eden Robinson, Annabel Lyon,
Lawrence Hill, Esi Edugyan, et désormais l'impressionnant
showman par excellence, Tomson Highway. Pensons aux
fines observations de Boyden sur l'oppression sociale, les
identités culturelles et le lieu; ou à la réflexion de Johnston

sur la rencontre tumultueuse de l'histoire et la fiction.
Tenons compte avec Laferrière des épreuves de l'exil et
des joies de la migrance; ou de l'éthique personnelle et
communautaire du récit autochtone que nous présente
Robinson. L'antiquité et le présent se réunissent dans la
conférence de Lyon au sujet du mode créatif de la fiction
historique. Hill plaide le besoin d'une conversation
informée sur la censure des livres. Et dans les pages
qui suivent, Highway défend de manière captivante
l'apprentissage libérateur et heureux *d'autres langues, de la
langue des autres*, y compris le langage de la musique.

Les conférences de la collection Kreisel abordent les
grandes questions qui nous concernent tous et toutes dans
la spécificité de notre vécu contemporain, peu importent
nos différences. Dans une intention de dialogue libre et
honnête, ces conférences reflètent l'ardeur et la profondeur
intellectuelles ainsi que l'humour et l'élégance des huit
auteurs extrêmement doués et présentés jusqu'ici.
Ces conférences publiques se consacrent annuellement à
perpétuer la mémoire du Professeur Henry Kreisel. Auteur,
professeur universitaire et Officier de l'Ordre du Canada,
Henry Kreisel est né à Vienne d'une famille juive en 1922.
En 1938, il a quitté son pays natal pour l'Angleterre et a
été interné pendant dix-huit mois, au Canada, lors de la
Deuxième Guerre mondiale. Après ses études à l'Université
de Toronto, il devint professeur à l'Université de l'Alberta
en 1947, et à partir de 1961 jusqu'à 1970, il a dirigé le
département d'anglais. De 1970 à 1975, il a été vice-recteur
(universitaire), et a été nommé professeur hors rang en
1975, la plus haute distinction scientifique décernée par
l'Université de l'Alberta à un membre de son professorat.
Professeur adoré, il a transmis l'amour de la littérature

à plusieurs générations d'étudiants, et il a été parmi
les premiers écrivains modernes du Canada à aborder
l'expérience immigrante. Il est décédé à Edmonton en
1991. Son œuvre comprend les romans, *The Rich Man* (1948)
et *The Betrayal* (1964), et un recueil de nouvelles intitulé
The Almost Meeting (1981). Son journal d'internement,
accompagné d'articles critiques sur ses écrits, paraît dans
Another Country: Writings By and About Henry Kreisel (1985).
La générosité du Professeur Kreisel est une source
d'inspiration profonde quant au travail public et
scientifique du clc de sonder la grande diversité et la
qualité remarquable des écrits du Canada. Le Centre adhère
à l'importance qu'accordait de façon inaugurale Henry
Kreisel à la connaissance des littératures de son propre
pays. Le clc poursuit une meilleure compréhension
d'un monde compliqué et difficile que peut réimaginer et
transformer la littérature.

Le Centre de littérature canadienne a été créé en
2006 grâce au don directeur du bibliophile illustre
edmontonien, le docteur Eric Schloss.

MARIE CARRIÈRE
Directrice, Centre de littérature canadienne
Edmonton, août 2014

NOTE
1. "Introduction," *A Tale of Monstrous Extravagance*, xiii.

INTRODUCTION

I MUST START by saying thank you Creator for this day, thank you Mother Earth for holding us, thank you grandfathers and mothers. Distinguished and honoured guests, thank you for coming. Please join me in recognizing that we gather on the traditional lands of Treaty 6 territory and of the Cree, Blackfoot and the Métis.

In this event we come together, listen with more than our ears, remove blinders and become part of the celebration, expand our thinking and feeling of inclusion, and build relationships.

My mother has always told me that "Culture is an imperative to action." It is not something we experience passively; it's what we give, what we do. Culture is what sustains the Aboriginal community and allows it to thrive— it is the best we have to offer society; it encompasses all our philosophies, our history, our knowledge, our experiences and skills, our humour, and perspectives. Culture is our guide to governance and process.

Arts began as participatory processes embedded in ceremonies that included dance, song, and drama, that communicated our humanity to the Creator. Sacred knowledge, histories, and cultural values were transmitted, and were instrumental in engaging community to make the arts conduits of energy, social criticism, and embodiments of vitality.

Art is a powerful medicine for the artist, the Aboriginal community, and the non-Aboriginal community because it builds the bridge to healthier relationships between each of us. This building of bridges is what we have come to celebrate in the company of Tomson Highway.

Tomson Highway was born in a snow bank on the Manitoba/Nunavut border to a family of nomadic caribou hunters. He had the great privilege of growing up in two languages, neither of which was French or English; they were Cree, his mother tongue, and Dene, the language of the neighbouring "nation," a people with whom they roamed and hunted. Today, he enjoys an international career as playwright, novelist, and pianist/songwriter. His best-known works are the plays *The Rez Sisters, Dry Lips Oughta Move to Kapuskasing, Rose, Ernestine Shuswap Gets Her Trout*, and the best-selling novel, *Kiss of the Fur Queen*. For many years, he ran Canada's premiere Native theatre company, Native Earth Performing Arts (based in Toronto), out of which has emerged an entire generation of professional Native playwrights, actors and, more indirectly, the many other Native theatre companies that now dot our country.

I am the artistic director of Alberta Aboriginal Performing Arts, a professional Theatre and Performing Arts organization. We encourage and inspire collaborations in art and performance in both contemporary and traditional styles and bring these creations to audiences across Alberta and around the world. We produce the Rubaboo Arts Festival.

As with most artists, it has been an incredible journey to get where I am today and whether he knows it or not, our esteemed friend Tomson Highway helped me and many other indigenous artists get here.

I first learned about Mr. Highway when a good friend of mine, Scott Sharplin, proposed to do his play *The Rez Sisters* at a community theatre here in Edmonton. Scott encountered quite a bit of pushback and resistance to producing this seminal work. The main arguments were:

- We don't have the Aboriginal talent pool to fill all the roles;
- We don't have an audience for an Aboriginal show; and
- We shouldn't do this because don't Aboriginal people want to own their stories.

Well, Scott argued back that there were a number of Aboriginal actors that he could personally name and many that might come to auditions—what a good way this would be to find out what the talent pool really consisted of. He argued further that the theatre had subscription holders and supporters even without marketing *The Rez Sisters* specifically. And finally, the theatre paid royalty rights, like you do with any playwright, so the question of ownership was already resolved. Furthermore, even though this may seem like a good intention, if we used our critical thinking capacity and followed that train of thought to its conclusion, we would realize that it meant only Aboriginal theatre companies could produce Aboriginal plays. With only about eight Aboriginal companies across Canada with the capacity to stage a play of this size, the work could very quickly become shelved and lifeless. I don't know of a single artist, Aboriginal or not, who wants only to be produced in a way that limits the life of their work. At its worst it is segregation.

I am very happy to report that the company went ahead and produced *The Rez Sisters* in 2005 and it became the first production in the fifty-year history of that company to get an entire run sold out. There were busloads of people coming in from out of town to see the show. There was so much buzz and support that we, the actors of the show, became the Old Earth Productions Collective and are now operating as a not-for-profit arts company. Old Earth Productions produced *The Rez Sisters* again as a Fringe show in 2006. And now they are creating new works. I also see that production as the beginning spark of Alberta Aboriginal Arts. So you see, at least two arts organizations came from one of Tomson Highway's plays. And that's just in Edmonton. My business partner in Alberta Aboriginal Arts, Ryan Cunningham, is now the Artistic Director of Native Earth in Toronto.

Last night Tomson asked me to keep this introduction short. He told me to let you know that he is related to, maybe even a descendant of, the Sasquatch; that he was born under a clothesline...that's where he still likes to hang! And then there are the stories of his family of circus performers!

Tomson Highway is the foundation of existing community relationships, the father of a renaissance in artistic practice and appreciation, and the resurgence and evolution of cultural knowledge.

All my relations. Hyi hyi. I present: Tomson Highway!

CHRISTINE SOKAYMOH FREDERICK
Edmonton, March 2014

PREAMBLE

TANSI, NIWEECHEEWAAGANUK, TANSI.
Kinanaaskoomitinaawow kaagithow keethawow
eetasee-eek oota kaapee-ik eepeen'toomiyeek tapee-
aachimoostaatag'wow oomsi isi anooch kaageesigaak.
Niweecheewaagan, Marie Carrière at'wayitha meena
ooma iskool University of Alberta kaa-iseetheegaateek
meena ooma ooteenow Edmonton kaa-ichigaateek,
keetheewow meena kinanaaskoomitinaawow.
Kinanaaskoomitinaawow meena Canadian Literature
Centre. Eric Schloss meena mista-i ninanaaskoomow,
athis ithigook isa kaageek'seewaat'sit, ithigook isa
kaageesaageetak ooma iskool. Kinanaaskoomitinaawow
kaagithow kaa-itasee-eek oota kaageepeen'toomiyeek
tapeegee-oogaatag'wow saasay meena oomsi isi. Kwayus
nimeeth'weetheeteen.

Bonsoir à tous, bonsoir à tout le monde. La première
chose que je voudrais vous dire avant de véritablement
commencer ma conférence c'est de vous remercier de
m'avoir invité à présenter cette conférence ici à l'Universite
d'Alberta, ici dans la belle ville d'Edmonton, ici dans la belle
province de l'Alberta. Je voudrais remercier surtout la belle

et super gentille Marie Carrière qui a travaillé tellement fort à organiser cet évènement, un évènement tellement spécial. La ville d'Edmonton a de la chance d'avoir quelqu'un comme Marie parmi ses citoyennes. Merci, Marie. Merci également au Centre de littérature canadienne. Et, finalement, un grand merci à Monsieur Eric Schloss, un vrai visionnaire pour avoir contribué d'une façon tellement réelle à la richesse culturelle et intellectuelle de cette ville. Je répète, un vrai visionnaire, ce Monsieur Schloss. C'est toujours un immense plaisir pour moi d'être ici, d'être avec vous, d'être parmi vous, ici dans une des institutions d'éducation les plus respectées et admirées au Canada et, finalement, au monde.

Good evening, ladies and gentlemen, good evening friends. The first thing I'd like to say before I start my lecture in earnest is to thank you all for inviting me to your beautiful city, especially the very kind and talented Marie Carrière who has worked so very hard to organize this event, who has worked so very hard at making sure that everything worked out just so. Edmonton should consider itself lucky to have such an asset in its midst. Chapeau Marie! Second, I would like to thank the Canadian Literature Centre for receiving me so kindly. And last, a huge thank you to Mr. Eric Schloss for having contributed in a manner so significant to this city. Always such a pleasure for me to come here and hang...

A Tale of
MONSTROUS
Extravagance

In fact, the land
that I speak of
was so far north
that Cree,
rightly speaking,
didn't even
belong there.

I WAS CONCEIVED, BORN, AND RAISED AT FOUR CORNERS.
Not Sudbury, Ontario's world-famous Four Corners, of
course, and certainly not the American town of Four
Corners, thus named for the reason that that is the only
place in the entire USA where meet four states, namely
Arizona, New Mexico, Utah, and Colorado. No, those are
not the Four Corners I speak of. I speak here of Canada's
own, one and only, and only very recently created Four
Corners, where, that is, now meet the provinces of
Manitoba and Saskatchewan and the Territories called
Northwest and Nunavut. Take that, Geography 101! Except
that, of course, Nunavut came into existence only in 1999
when I was already forty-seven, but that's another story...

Northern Manitoba, in any case, is where I come from.
Unfortunately for those of us who come from the area,
when people think northern Manitoba, they envision, in
a flash, the port town of Churchill on the Hudson's Bay.
But no, that's not where I come from. I come, quite on
the other hand, from the province's other end, that is, its

western extremity, so far west of Churchill that it—that is, Churchill—might as well be, to us, a suburb of Minsk, Belarus. And Winnipeg so far south that, to us, it might as well be a beach in Rio de Janeiro. Even the mining town of Thompson was, for us, as exotic and remote as Managua, Nicaragua. So far north is the land that I come from, in fact, that, back in the day when I was born—which, of course, takes us back to the era of Ghengis Khan and his wife Agnes—European languages of any kind whatsoever were unheard of. English wasn't spoken, French wasn't spoken, even Ukrainian was a complete non-presence. The only human languages that were heard and spoken up in those parts back in those days were Aboriginal, and of these there were three: Dene, Cree, and Inuktituk. In fact, the land that I speak of was so far north that Cree, rightly speaking, didn't even belong there. Rightly speaking, this, the land that straddles the northern extremity of the three Prairie provinces and the southern extremities of the Northwest, Nunavut, and Yukon Territories, was Dene territory. Cree, by comparison, came, as it still does, from the south, relatively speaking, from the central portion of the three Prairie provinces. And, of course, the northern halves of Ontario and Québec.

My father, Joe Highway—may he rest in peace—came from a First Nation called Pelican Narrows which lies just inside Saskatchewan from Manitoba and some hundred kilometres north and slightly west of the border mining town of Flin Flon, Manitoba. As a young man not yet twenty, he went to work as an oarsman for the York boats sent to the far north by the Hudson's Bay Company to trade with the Indians. And when he laid eyes for the first time on the barren lands at the southern edge of what was then still just the Northwest Territories, he was smitten. And that was that. At that point in his life, he became a northern Manitoban and stayed so for the rest of his life. The First Nation of which he eventually became a registered member, the Barren Lands First Nation—the territory of which is called Barren Lands, the village of which is called Brochet (pronounced "Bro-shay")—lay not quite in the barrens of Nunavut. It lay just south of them, just inside, that is, the province of Manitoba where it also meets his native Saskatchewan. And though we had a house in the village of Brochet, we, in reality, spent very little time there. Where we did spend time was out on the land, a remarkable land, a beautiful land, a land not seen to this day by the most adventurous of Europeans, whether fur trader, missionary, prospector, cartographer, or Avon saleswoman. It was a land populated by great herds of caribou and filled to surfeit by a thousand crystal-watered lakes, with ten thousand islands ringed by beaches as stunning as Brazil's and rivers and waterfalls and eskers and very low forest of spruce and pine and birch and willow. And by Dene, an Athapaskan-speaking people whose presence on that land goes back eons. This made the twelve brown offspring of Joe and Pelagie Highway Cree Indian children who had the privilege of growing up in Dene territory *with* Dene children. It made us bilingual right from birth, the older children more so than the youngest, for I am but the eleventh of the twelve.

As a nomadic people, our wanderings varied. There were years, for example, when we travelled further north, always by dogsled in winter, canoe in summer. And then there were years when we stayed closer to our home base of Brochet. In fact, before I was born, that is to say, when

my parents were younger, had fewer children, and thus
were more mobile, those wanderings sometimes took us
so far north that we were beyond Manitoba and well into
Nunavut, where we met and mingled with yet another
Aboriginal people, the peaceful Inuit with their sealskin
costumes, their houses made of ice, and their own dances
such as...the twist. In this way, their language entered
our lexicon. Inuktituk this language is called. In fact, so
close did our lives eventually intertwine with theirs that
intermarriage happened on a basis semi-regular, resulting
in the fact that, to this day, I have relatives who are part
Inuit. And so Inuktituk was heard, when I was growing up,
right there in Brochet. So there we were, Joe and Pelagie
Highway's brood, the privileged children of three Native
languages each as distinct one from the other as English
is from Arabic and Korean or French is from Mandarin

So there we were,
Joe and Pelagie
Highway's brood,
the privileged
children of three
Native languages
each as distinct
one from the
other as English is
from Arabic... ⁝

⋮ In fact, the first European language that I was to learn, as it turns out, was neither. It was Latin, whereby hangs a tale of monstrous extravagance...

or Swahili—for Cree, like Ojibway and Blackfoot, is an Algonquian language; Dene, like Slavey and Dogrib, Athapaskan; and Inuktituk resides in a linguistic family all on its own, like Hungarian in Europe, let us say. Between these three Native languages, that is to say, there is not a stitch of similarity, not a syllable in common. And English was to come much later, as was French. In fact, the first European language that I was to learn, as it turns out, was neither. It was Latin, whereby hangs a tale of monstrous extravagance...

Be that as it may, if we were bilingual in Cree and Dene, then so was Brochet. At the north end of this village that never numbered more than 800 people lived the status Cree. At its south, the non-status Cree (as if being Cree to begin with was not complicated enough already!). In between these two split communities lived the Dene. Just to cross from one side of the village to the other—for we were status who happened to have relatives who had married non-status—one had to change language not once but twice: once from Cree to Dene when we walked through the Dene neighbourhood and the dogs barked at us in Dene and we had to bark back in Dene, and once from Dene back to Cree when we reached the other side. By the time you arrived at your Aunt Emily's, your tongue was exhausted. Changing linguistic gears on a dime like that will do that to you. And speaking of Aunt Emily, she was half Dene, for my mother's father, when he lost his first wife to death by illness, took on a Dene woman as a second wife and from that union had this Aunt Emily and five other children. Intermarriage between the Cree and the Dene, that is to say, transpired with a regularity that, as the years moved forward, alarmed race purists and sparked wild rumours.

As you may have read, or may not have read, on the Internet, I was born in a snow bank. In the dead of a Manitoba winter, which sounds extraordinary, if not quite fictive. Wild exaggeration is the term I've been accused of when recounting this chapter of my life. But where those vile insinuations come from is that ninety per cent of Canadians reside in that very narrow strip of land that hugs the American border, so they know very little about the true north strong and free. Because the truth of the matter is that, back in the 50s when I was born—and in the 40s, 30s, and back to the cave days—not all but many, many people were born like that, in, that is, such magic circumstances, circumstances, that is, when men talked to animals and trees talked to women. It was par for the course. We're a northern people. Northerners are an extraordinary people who were born on an extraordinary land. I mean, not much further north of us, for god's sake, people were born in houses made of ice—they're called igloos—and people were born on ice floes which, in their own way, are icebergs of sorts. I mean, imagine being able to say that you were born on an iceberg. The tale of being born in a snow bank pales by comparison.

But what actually happened was that I was born in a tent *pitched* in a snow bank in one awful hurry as my family, as usual, was traversing the tundra by dogsled, this some 100 kilometres north of Brochet—that is to say, in the very heart of Dene territory. And because this was the case, a Dene encampment just happened to be close by, which was why an old Dene woman named Titty Ray Loorah was roped into caring for my mother in her sickbed (sorry about the "Titty Ray," folks, but Dene names have always stumped me when it comes to their spelling in Roman orthography as the language isn't written, so this is the best I can do). And as my mother, as did my father, spoke fluent Cree *and* fluent Dene, she and this midwife, Titty Ray Loorah, would have communicated in Dene so that the first words I heard when I came into this world were not English, not French, not Cree but, of all things, Dene.

The Dene language belongs to the Earth, it comes from the Earth, it sounds like the Earth: goosigaal (come here); yooway sanathere (go over there); sagans-choo (give me some, but only in the context of food); koosiles-si (I don't know); bagine-deleh (never mind); "eh" for "yes," "eeleh" for "no"; noria (imagine!); koos'thleh (good grief); even dice-leenee bay-yaazay (its most common swear word, which I will not translate). I still remember significant amounts of it though I rarely speak it these days. And with names like Denetchezhe, Tssazze, Dantouze, Gazayou,

Adoonaazay, Jalak-waazay, Old Dice Chagaazay, etc., the
letter "z" lies close to its centre. It is the sound that anchors
it where, on the other hand, the "z" is completely absent in
Cree, which is more in love with the "k" and the "ch," as in
"kipoochim" and the "p" as in "papagoowa-yaan." So if the
Dene language belongs to and comes from the soil and the
muskeg and the reindeer moss of the northern extremities
of the three Prairie provinces and a sizeable chunk of the
Northwest Territories—though not so much Nunavut for,
on that side, the language merely peeks into is southern
extremity—then Cree comes from the laughter of a cosmic
clown, as he/she has been called, a merry-maker called the
Trickster, Weesageechaak in Cree, Nanabush in Ojibway,
Glooscap in Mi'kmaq, Iktomi in Lakota, Coyote on the
plains, Raven on the west coast. He/she goes by many
names and comes in many guises, which is why Cree has
got to be the world's funniest language. I lie not when I
say that each syllable is a kick in the pants, a poke in the

...then Cree
comes from the
laughter of a
cosmic clown, as
he/she has been
called, a merry-
maker called the
Trickster...

⁝ A Hail Mary contest, my dear friends and colleagues, is when the entire population of a village like Brochet kneels in a row on the main street with their rosaries jangling and rattling in their hands like the chains of love.

bum, a quality not helped by the fact that my dialect of the language also happens to be the fastest of any dialect of any language anywhere on the planet.

So now, very briefly, I'll take a dip into its rhythm and character. Fasten your chastity belts, ladies and gentlemen, it's gonna be a bumpy ride. You see, Brochet, unfortunately, was converted in the late nineteenth century by French Roman Catholic missionaries so that, to this day, the fastest Hail Mary in the world is heard there. My mother—may she rest in peace—used to say her rosaries with such blinding speed that sparks could be seen flying out of her

mouth on a basis semi-regular and, one day, set the priest
on fire in the confessional! Which is where the expression
"Holy smoke!" comes from, for that's exactly what the
priest said. "Holy smoke!" he ejaculated, "My cassock's on
fire!" And then you know what happened? The Brochet
fire department pulled up in a cloud of dust and doused
him with holy water. That's how Catholic Brochet was
at the time. Ever heard of a Hail Mary contest? Do you
have Hail Mary contests in Edmonton? No? Shame on
you. And you consider yourselves good Christians! You
wanna know what a Hail Mary contest is? A Hail Mary
contest, my dear friends and colleagues, is when the entire
population of a village like Brochet kneels in a row on the
main street with their rosaries jangling and rattling in
their hands like the chains of love. Then the priest shoots a
handgun—BANG! And the people go signing the Cross and
rattling off their Hail Marys: Kitatamiskaatin Marie, seeya
kaskiniskaakooyaan manto-saakeehitoowin, kitiheek ayow
K'simanto. Ispichi kaakithow iskweewuk keetha athiwak
kititi-theetaakoosin athiwak meena iteetheetaakoosin
Jesoos kaakikikiskawat. Kichitwaa-Marie K'simanto
oogaaweemis aya-meestamawinaan, piyaastaahooyaak,
anooch meena weenpiyaagi. Pitanigooseegik. And they end
with another signing of the Cross.

You see? I just won the Hail Mary contest. Gimme
twenty bucks.

Peeyak keeskichithow-asaagay, neesoo keeskichithow-
asaagaya, n'stoo keeskichithow-asaagaya. You see, you don't
even know what I'm saying but you're laughing already—
or at least smiling—and all I'm saying is "one skirt, two
skirts, three skirts." Or rather, in literal translation, one
dress cut in half, two dresses cut in half, three dresses cut

in half..." because that, after all, is what a skirt is: a dress cut in half. That's how comical the syllables are in Cree.

I'll give you three more examples.

I will conjugate the verb *to breathe*: n'pagitataamoon, kipagitataamoon, pagitataamoo, n'pagitataamoonaan, kipagitataamoonaawow, pagitataamoowuk.

I will conjugate the verb *to suffer*: nigagwaatageetaan, kigagwaatageeetaan, kagwaatageetow, nigagwaatageetaanaan, kigagwaatageeetaanaawow, kagwaatageetaawuk. You see? Even the verb *to suffer* is funny! It's all, as I say, in the syllables.

Now I will conjugate the verb *to go sour*: niweecheegipathin, kiweecheegipathin, weecheegipathoo, niweecheegipathinaan, kiweecheegipathinaawow, weecheegipathoowuk.

And last I will say a simple phrase: neeeeeeee, awinak awa oota kaapeepeetigweet? In Cree, it's hysterical. We laugh and laugh and laugh when we say it when, in fact, all I'm saying translates into English as, "Hey, who just came in the door?" Now I ask you: is that funny? Indubitably and categorically *not*. I tell you, if air traffic control at airports functioned in Cree, no plane would ever make it to the tarmac. The pilots and the people in the air traffic control tower would be laughing so hard they'd forget their instruments and kill ten thousand. So no, no laughter at the airport, please. I want to get home.

Aside from humour, however, there are other, even more significant, differences between Cree and Dene on the one hand, and French and English on the other, between, that is, Aboriginal languages and their European counterparts, keeping in mind that I am nominally familiar with at least one other in the former category, namely Ojibway, and with at least four others in the latter, among them Spanish and German. But the fundamental difference has to do with gender and its immediate offshoot, namely the aliveness—or deadness—of nature.

European languages are obsessed by the question of gender. They divide the universe into that which is male and that which is female—in English less so than in French or German, say, but the division is still there. In the monotheistic superstructure that they define, God is Male with a capital *M*, then there is male with a small *m*, followed by female with a small *f*, followed by nature—and hell, for that matter—which are genderless. They are, in other words, "its." Now, the question students always ask me is: where, in this superstructure, is Female with a capital *F*? The answer?

...European languages are obsessed by the question of gender. They divide the universe into that which is male and that which is female... ⁝

⁝ Aboriginal languages, on the other hand, divide their universe not into genders but into that which is animate and that which is inanimate...

Nowhere. There is no such thing as Female with a capital F in such a design. Because this design, in the final analysis, is a phallic superstructure, a hierarchic straight line that goes from God as Male at the top to male to female to neuter at the bottom, with one level of power having complete and utter power over the next. And there is room for two genders only, with one at the complete mercy of the other. And god help the person who tries to cross that gender divide.

Aboriginal languages, on the other hand, divide their universe not into genders but into that which is animate and that which is inanimate—things, that is, that have a soul and things that do not. The gender or a hierarchy thereof has no significance. We are all, when all is said and done, he/shes, as is God, one would think. The resulting superstructure is thus not the straight line of monotheism but the circle, the womb of pantheism, a system wherein God *is* nature, God is biology, God is the land. A yonic superstructure, that is to say, as opposed to one that is phallic. It is a design, in other words, where there is room—and plenty of it—for the notion of God as Female *and* for more than just two genders. And so goes the argument.

Just to avoid another case of our late Cree sister, Helen Betty Osborne, who was murdered by being stabbed in the vagina fifty-six times with a screwdriver, to avoid another case of Robert Pickton and his twenty-nine victims, to avoid another Prince-George-to-Prince-Rupert Highway of Tears where dozens of Native women continue to be murdered in cold blood, we need fifty-six genders, to my way of thinking, if only to honour those fifty-six legendary screwdriver stabs.

A woman, according to the Aboriginal system, is animate, she has a soul (ana iskwew, the article *ana* being the operative principle, the *le* or *la* in French, the *der, die,* or *das* in German); a man has a soul (ana naapew); as does a tree (ana seeti) a cow (ana moostoos), and a rock (ana asini). All *ana*s, so to speak, have a place of equality on that circle of living, breathing beings. And the only way you can make them inanimate is to remove their souls so that a woman who has died automatically becomes "anima meeyow" (the corpse). Ditto for the man. The dead tree is made into a chair (anima teetapoowin), making that chair a tree without a soul; the dead cow is made into a roast (anima weeyaas), the rock is crushed into cement and made into a sidewalk transforming that sidewalk (anima meeskanow) into a rock without a soul—the operative word in all this being the article *anima*. And because the straight line of heaven to hell exists not, all these dead don't go to either. Once they die, they merely get "translated" into another form of energy where they migrate to another part of that same circle. This is why the Earth is such a magical place: because the dead—your brother, your sister, mother, father, grandmother, grandfather, son, daughter, best friend, all of whom are gone—are still here with us not as a ghost but as blade of grass, leaf of tree, ray of sunshine, a warm summer breeze, the blood in your veins, a certain vibration. And biology—not man but the planet—has pride of place in the great scheme of things. And so goes the argument.

Now let's take this equation of animate/inanimate one level deeper. All the parts of the human body, by themselves, are inanimate. The head by itself (anima mistigwaan) has no soul—you will notice that the article *ana* has now been replaced by the article *anima*; the hand (anima micheechee) has no gender and neither does the leg (anima ooskaat), the stomach (anima watay), or the bladder (anima weekwi). Even the heart by itself is soulless (anima ootee). The penis? Dead as a doorknob, sorry boys. The only parts of the human body that, by themselves, have a soul are the vagina and the womb, which is where the concept of God as female rests rock solid, which is where the Female with the capital F belongs, right smack in the centre of that yonic circle.

But then there is one other organ that, because of the nature of the English language, I am forbidden from telling you about, an organ that, by itself, has a soul. You'll just have to guess which one it is. Here are some clues. First, both men and women have it. Second, European languages were evicted from a certain garden—the garden of joy, the garden of beauty, the garden of pleasure—at a certain point in their emotional history. Aboriginal mythology/

theology has no such narrative—to them therefore
northern Alberta is still a garden. And that other human
organ that, by itself, has a soul, lives in the centre of the
original garden, in, that is, the human body. Third, it is the
human body's funniest, most ridiculous-looking part, the
birthplace of the Trickster, that cosmic clown. You might
hear it tonight as you're brushing your teeth. In English, it
will disgust you because the garden, finally, is disgusting.
In Cree, you will laugh until you weep. All right, I'll release
you from your misery—that third organ is the anus. Ever
hear a fart?...In Aboriginal mythology, wonder of wonders,
this is where the concept arises of a female god who laughs.
And laughs and laughs and laughs.

Don't let any of this upset or even scare you, ladies and
gentlemen. Cree is a dying language. English will live
on forever. Long live God as Male. And death to all other
genders. Death to the Earth.

Without speaking other languages, you would *never*
know these facts. You would *never* know that such a vision
of life, one so different from yours, existed. There is simply

Speaking one
language,
I submit,
is like living
in a house
with one
window... ⦂

Needless to say, however—that is, back in my days as a boy soprano— I loved wrapping my hot little tongue around some good, hot Latin.

no other way of digging out such information. Speaking one language, I submit, is like living in a house with one window only; all you see is that one perspective when, in point of fact, dozens, hundreds, of other perspectives exist and one must, at the very least, heed them, see them, hear them.

At age almost seven I left the paradise that is northern Manitoba to go to boarding school. That's what I call it because, for me, it was a positive experience. Because of the practically Jesuit-style regimented education that I got at that school, for one thing, I enjoy today a thriving international career that takes me, regular as clockwork, to all six inhabited continents—I just got back from India and I'm on my way to Brazil. Goodbye -30. Don't get me wrong. I say "I left paradise" but the truth is that it was only for ten months of every year. The two months of summer? They were so spectacular that they more than replaced the other ten months, especially with parents as remarkable as ours. As a boy of eleven fishing commercially with his dad from three in the morning to six in the evening—just the two of us in the canoe, two elder brothers manning another, brothers-in-law and whatnot manning a third and with Sunday as our one day off a week—I got to spend more time with this fantastic man, Joe Highway, in just one summer, than the richest white boy in Rosedale gets to spend with his in a lifetime.

But back to that school. It was, of course, a Catholic school and, being a boy aged six-going-on-seven, I was pressed into service as an altar boy. This is the late 1950s going into the early 1960s that we speak of, before the Second Vatican Council of 1962 transpired wherein the Pope changed the liturgy from one said in Latin to one said in the vernacular of whatever country. I was ten already when that Council happened so that I had already gotten, to my immense pleasure, to learn all that gorgeous Latin, all that gorgeous Gregorian chanting. I still know it: Dominus vobiscum. Et cum spiritu tuo. Per omnia saecula saeculorum. Amen. "Dominus vobiscum" means "the Lord be with you"; "Et cum spiritu tuo" means "and with your spirit, too"; "Per omnia saecula saeculorum" means "forever and ever." And "Amen," of course, means, "you got that right, baby." The Asperges Me, the Sanctus, the Agnus Dei, the Credo, the Tantum Ergo, we sang it all. And back then I had a voice that was sweeter than honey, high as a piccolo, for I was, you see, a boy soprano and because I was musical...well...I sang so well that they seriously considered turning me into a castrato when I turned twelve. It is indeed unfortunate that they didn't because, today, I have a voice that makes blood curdle. I mean, if your dear k.d. lang has a voice that brings a lump to people's throats, as they say it does, I have one that brings a lunch to people's throats. Needless to say, however—that is, back in my days as a boy soprano—I loved wrapping my hot little tongue around some good, hot Latin. I still do...whenever I'm in Rome, or Rio de Janeiro, neeee...

And *then* after Latin I finally encountered English full force. "See Spot run. See David come. All over Spot. Run Spot run. Run, run, run." Again, I had a gas, even though, much later on, once I got out of the sheltered atmosphere of boarding school with what amounted to 200 siblings— that is, my schoolmates—whom I loved, and still do, with all my heart, once I left the supportive atmosphere of my own family and once I ended up in high school in Winnipeg, it turned out to be an exercise in rank and dreadful embarrassment. All-out humiliation. As it turns out, the English that we had learned among ourselves at that boarding school was a pidgin English that belonged only and exclusively to that isolated place way out in the bush some thirty kilometres north of the railway town of The Pas, Manitoba: "Neeee, never saw, it don't sounds good, you want some the coffee, my father he want some gazzy, hey, hey, hey, hey, hey, I saw you stoling," that sort of thing. Well, that just didn't cut it in this big white city which was, like it or not, my new home and hearth. Still, I swallowed my hurt, my pride, and my sorrow, wiped off my tears, and soldiered on. And with the help of many remarkable, kind, and very generous white people, right up to my years in university *and* beyond, I eventually mastered it until I could speak it like good Queen Elizabeth away over there across *keechigamaak*, as we call the Atlantic Ocean—that is, "the Great Water"—in Cree. Learning another language, it's like that—humiliating as hell. You get laughed at for the mistakes that you make, you get mocked for your accent, you just get laughed at, but you don't let it stop you. You just grit your teeth and march on forward.

Fortunately, I had the privilege of learning yet another language at the same time as I did English, and this language was music. I had picked up the piano at that boarding school and once I was in high school in Winnipeg, Indian Affairs, god bless them, always made sure they boarded me at a home that had a piano for I was obsessed with the instrument. My paternal grandfather was a legendary fiddler, my father played the accordion, so I, third generation in this line of musicians, would become a pianist. It was a natural progression. In those days, high school in Manitoba didn't offer music as an elective, so all music lessons, if one wanted them, had to be taken outside school hours. They were considered, that is to say, extracurricular activity.

My paternal grandfather was a legendary fiddler, my father played the accordion, so I, third generation in this line of musicians, would become a pianist.

⋮ Music, as it turns
out, is the original
and only universal
language, the only
one understood
and spoken in all
195 countries on
this planet.

Now I don't have my facts dead-on, but at 7 A.M. Monday
morning, say, I would be at my private lesson in harmony
chez Gwen Davies, this eccentric old woman who walked
with a cane. At 7 A.M. Tuesday, I was at my lesson in form.
7 A.M. Wednesday, it was my lesson in history—that is,
music history. 7 A.M. Thursday, I was at my lesson in
counterpoint. Etcetera. And this, keep in mind, entailed
my getting up at 5:30 A.M. every morning to get on a bus
in the butt-freezing winter of Winnipeg to cross the city
and then cross it going the other way to be at school in
time for 9. And then blessed Saturday was the day of my
weekly piano lesson. Heaven. In this way—and later on at
university— I learned to deconstruct and then reconstruct
a Beethoven sonata, to play Chopin Nocturnes, to write my
own fugue in the style of Bach, to write for an orchestra, to
play the chamber music of Mendelssohn, Schubert, and
Shostakovich, to accompany opera singers and, in the

process, familiarize myself with the operatic repertoire, etc. From age eighteen to age twenty-two, that's all I did. It was total immersion. I was a Buddhist monk and music was my god. I may not quite have reached my dream of becoming a concert pianist—I started too late, was born in the wrong place at the right time: northern Manitoba in a snow bank, with the nearest piano 500 kilometres away. I mean, Glenn Gould was born in Toronto, Martha Argerich in Buenos Aires, Evgeny Kissin in Moscow, Yuja Wang in Beijing, Jan Lisiecki in Calgary. All these good people, god bless them, born and raised in the music capitals, if not of the world then of their respective countries. *They* were born in the right place at the right time but *I* wasn't, so I had no choice but to move on to other dreams which, god willing, I had a-plenty, one of which was to write my own music for my own shows; another of which was to write songs, and play them, for my own cabarets, cabarets that are now heard on six continents. Music, as it turns out, is the original and only universal language, the only one understood and spoken in all 195 countries on this planet.

One definition of musical literacy—and there are many definitions—is to be able to read a line of music. It's very simple. Do you know the difference between a C:

And a G:

There are five notes between them. That's called an interval of a perfect fifth. A perfect fifth is an interval of five notes between two notes:

A major third is the note halfway between the notes of the perfect fifth, which is formed in this case by the E natural, so that the three notes played together — the tonic, the third and the dominant — form a chord, the C major chord:

From the C major chord we progress to the C 7th. That's adding the minor 7th, the B flat. In doing so, you colour it. It's like painting a...painting. But if you take that B flat up one semi-tone to the B natural, you get a C major 7th:

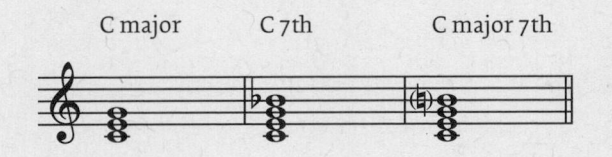

And if you take that major 7th down to a major 6th, that is, change the B natural at the top to an A natural, then you end up with the C 6th chord:

Take that up a perfect fourth—four notes between them—you find yourself in the key of F, and it changes:

Music has colour. They say that F is blue. They say that G major is yellow. They say that A minor is black. D flat major is pink. When you hear a Sonata in D flat major, for instance, it's dreamy, dreamy stuff.

This is the F with a major 7th:

Alternate it with a major 6th, which in this case is the D:

Music has colour. They say that F is blue. They say that G major is yellow. They say that A minor is black. D flat major is pink.

⁞ Dig out the biographical details of the most successful men and women on Earth...and you will find, almost always, in that biography, the essential element of that sixth sense: musical literacy.

You alternate these notes and then you add the element of rhythm, the bass, you add syncopation, and then you add the melody.... From there, you're set to play an entire piece.

To be able to distinguish these notes, to be able to talk like this, to know exactly what is happening mechanically in music and to know the psychological effect those sounds have on the human brain—thanks to intellectuals like Daniel Leviton, whose books you must read—is truly wonderful. It is to realize that music is a language with its own history and to know that what I've learned about all these fabulous composers and to know the history of music is a privilege.

Ludwig van Beethoven, god bless his genius, wrote thirty-two piano sonatas, the last three of which are, in order, written in E major (Opus 109), A flat major (Opus

110), and C minor (Opus 111). The third movement of the Opus 109, my favourite, is a theme and variations based on a simple tune.

To be able to talk intelligently and in an informed fashion about, say, the structure of Maurice Ravel's spectacular piano suite, *Gaspard de la Nuit* with its three pieces entitled *Ondine*, *Le Gibet*, and *Scarbo*, to know the intimate details of Johannes Brahms's great piano concerto in B flat major, or to talk of Chopin, Rachmaninoff, Scriabin, Verdi, Puccini, or Bellini gives you a perspective on the world and on life that is achievable in no other way. It is, that is to say, yet another window on another wall of that house. Dig out the biographical details of the most successful men and women on Earth—doctors, scientists, educators, politicians, architects, you name it—and you will find, almost always, in that biography, the essential element of that sixth sense: musical literacy. Once you have it, chances are—not always but almost—that you become a powerhouse, a real contender...

Donc, à un moment donné, j'ai commencé à parler français. Je ne me souviens pas exactement quand, mais j'avais commencé sans le savoir. C'était peut-être avec les religieuses au pensionnat où je suis allé. C'était peut-être avec des amis franco-manitobains que j'ai rencontrés à Winnipeg, où je suis allé à l'école secondaire. Et c'était certainement à Montréal une fois que j'avais commencé mes études à l'université à London, Ontario, car on allait de temps en temps à Montréal pour rendre visite à de chers amis, des amis que j'adorais. Et plus tard en France, où je suis allé la première fois à l'âge de vingt ans et où j'ai vécu de l'âge de quarante-huit ans jusqu'à l'année passée, c'est-à-dire à l'âge de soixante-et-un ans, c'est-à-dire treize ans en tout. Mais je devrais continuer mon discours en anglais parce que, autrement, la plupart de mes chers amis dans cette belle salle ne comprendraient pas, mon dieu seigneur, comme ils disent au Québec, oh là là, comme ils disent en France. Mais quand même...what I just said was that I should continue my speech in English or I risk having my speech completely misunderstood. Or *un*-understood.

En tout cas. I started, at one point—I don't remember exactly when—learning French. I had, of course, heard it spoken by the nuns and priests and lay personnel at the boarding school I went to for they were almost all francophone. And then I studied the language, after a fashion, in high school in Winnipeg and lived and mingled with the Franco-Manitobans whose farms and villages surround Winnipeg. And then, later on in life, I took courses at places like l'Alliance Française, the University of Toronto, the Bouchereau International School of Languages in Montreal, spent tons of time in that city over the years and went—à maintes reprises—to France, including fun jags in Paris. And then later, had the great, good fortune to fall in love with a Franco-Ontarian, thus ending up moving into the heart of the Franco-Ontarian community around Sudbury, Ontario, from where he came and, later, moved to France with him. For thirteen years—or rather for the six winter months of every year for those thirteen years—I lived in a small seaside village in the south of France where my partner and I made dozens of friends and became part and parcel of entire families. My partner being an international-level bridge player, he, among other things, taught bridge to the elderly—of which, of course, France is not short of...and, in this way, we connected with the community not just in the village but also in those up and

down that part of the Mediterranean coast, from the city of
Perpignan to the country's border with Spain. And we were
loved and loved dearly and I was helped with my French —
the language being my partner's mother tongue, he needed
not the help that I did but, still, for those thirteen years, the
laughter at my mistakes? The subtle, tongue-in-cheek
mocking of my accent?

The French, for one thing, don't seem to understand that
no one but they will *ever* speak their language with their
accent and that they should accept this. They should accept —
and understand — that making the very arduous and painful
effort of learning their language is an act of respect for
their culture, an act of admiration, an act of love. Yes, it

They should
accept—and
understand—that
making the very
arduous and
painful effort of
learning their
language is an act
of respect for their
culture, an act of
admiration,
an act of love. ⸭

⋮ ...I would even
venture to say that
forcing your own
one language down
another person's
throat is not entirely
unlike breaking into
his house and
stealing his spirit.

means you love them. The question is: do *they* love *you?* For
a people so intelligent, so well-educated, so forward-
thinking, so sophisticated, I was surprised and dismayed
by how adamantly unilingual they are, though of course I
love them dearly so I can't exactly trash them now, can I!
But I read things like Agatha Christie in French translation
because they are formulaic and thus easy to understand.
Then I moved on to English classics that we all, here in
Canada, know well—books like *Oliver Twist*, in French
translation. Then I moved on to the French classics
themselves, Dumas, Zola, Balzac. In this way, I learned to
speak the language without fear and loathing.

And then because we lived in what, in effect, was the
French–Spanish border—where the Pyrenees plunge into
the Mediterranean—we spent tons of time in the villages
and cities of that part of Spain including, most especially,

the legendary city of Barcelona. There I picked up Spanish, etc., etc., etc.... So that's—what?—five, six languages? Take that, Rosedale!

The privilege of having grown up in three languages is that it gives you, in later life, the ability to absorb other languages like a sponge. There is, you see, a muscle, or a network of muscles, in the brain that was put there for the purpose of absorbing sound, as in sound waves, as in sonic vibrations. Musicians have the privilege of exercising that muscle—trust me, I used to have to memorize pages and pages of scores by Bach, Schumann, Scriabin, even the twelve-tone composer, Arnold Schoenberg. Ever seen a score by Arnold Schoenberg? Learning Chinese would be easier. But human language, too, is sound and sound waves and sonic vibration. And the earlier you put that muscle, or network of muscles, to work, the stronger it becomes. Like a gymnast's body, it grows in suppleness and dexterity. Four-year-olds, for instance, learn other languages just like that, with flawless accents. If you don't exercise that muscle it atrophies like any other muscle, so that if you're unilingual by age forty, then you're pretty well cursed to being unilingual for the rest of your life, *unless*, of course, you make an extraordinary effort to overcome that handicap. Which you should because—and there are studies to prove this—the exercise of that muscle in the brain staves off Alzheimer's. It is, after all, about the training of memory. It is like taking that muscle for a jog every day. Think of that as you're caring for your ninety-year-old widowed mother in that nursing home. Think of yourself at that age.

Not only is speaking one language like living in a house that has but one window, as I said earlier, it is like sitting at a dinner table where you do all the talking and you talk about nothing but yourself. It means you're not listening to what the other person has to say. It means you are not interested. And that's not good for relationships. In fact, I would even venture to say that forcing your own *one* language down another person's throat is not entirely unlike breaking into his house and stealing his spirit. I'm sorry, but having been at the receiving end of such aggression, *that's* what it feels like. It also has to do with style. Either you have style or you don't. Speaking only one language is like wearing the same grey coat day in and day out. It's boring. *You're* boring. You want to be able to change colours every day. You want to be able to flash your ass. But seriously, if a gay Cree Indian born in a snow bank on the Manitoba/Nunavut border with all the disadvantages that that would seem to entail at first glance...if such a person can master English until his tongue turned purple and can learn French to the point of total and abject humiliation *and* can learn to play Chopin like Itzhak Perlman plays Mrs. Perlman, then anyone—*anyone*—can learn three languages.

The question being: where do you learn them, these other languages? The school is called world travel. Go spend a year in Ecuador and pick up Spanish. It's a stunning country; hiking the Andes is one of life's great pleasures. Yes, make a fool of yourself and turn pink/purple but learn to say, "Muchisima gracias y hasta mañana, mi cariño." Or go to Spain or Argentina where, in the latter country, a decent hotel room costs the equivalent of $15 Canadian a night, a bottle of good red wine in a restaurant as low as $3, a one-way bus ticket from Edmonton to Calgary, or an equivalent distance thereof, costs $10 as opposed to $60. Go and live in the south of France for thirteen years, like we did, and become fluent in French (and drink red wine for $2.30 Canadian, I kid you not). Even Gaspé, Québec—without the wine, of course—would do the trick. Some people go to Japan to master Japanese, Russia to master Russian, Kuwait or Dubai to master Arabic, Rome or Florence to master Italian, and then find work in diplomatic fields such as embassies and consulates which are scattered all over the world, not to mention banks and international enterprises who need translators. Your ten-year-old daughter, if encouraged, if given the right tools now—like, today—can realistically become, by age fifty, Canada's ambassador to Hungary (Budapest is a fabulous city), Canada's ambassador to Chile

Statement, exhortation, plea: it is our responsibility as citizens of this stunning country, this privileged land, to hold it together, to make sure it doesn't fall apart. ⋮

⋮ Alors, multilingualism is the greatest gift you can give your child...

(Santiago is a fabulous city), Canada's ambassador to Japan (Tokyo is a fabulous city). Your child's life, that is to say, becomes that much richer, that much more fun, that much more colourful. And, most important, she will aid in the process of bringing the world together, of helping in the nurturing of world peace and stability—certainly *that* between Québec and the rest of Canada. Statement, exhortation, plea: it is our responsibility as citizens of this stunning country, this privileged land, to hold it together, to make sure it doesn't fall apart.

Alors, multilingualism is the greatest gift you can give your child because, in doing so, you give them the world, you give them a spectacular life, you give them one of the great keys to happiness. Trust me, I've been there. I am living proof. Come with me to Rio de Janeiro in two short weeks and I will show you the meaning of the words "good time."

Alors, le temps est venu de terminer ma présentation. J'espère que vous avez appris certaines choses, j'espère que j'ai réussi à ouvrir vos yeux, vos esprits et vos cœurs, à certaines nouvelles perspectives sur notre vie ici au Canada, sur notre culture comme Amérindiens, les résidents originaux de ce territoire. Encore, merci de m'avoir invité,

de m'avoir écouté tellement respectueusement. Merci d'être
venus, merci d'être là, merci d'être vous. Ce fut un honneur,
un immense plaisir. Mille mercis. Et bonne fin de soirée.

Keetawm kinanaaskoomitinaawow kaagithow
keethawow kaa-itasee-eek oota anooch kaatip'skaak athis
eegeepeentoomee-ik tapapeeskweetagwow oomisi isi.
Kwayus nigeemeeth'weetheeteen poog'weesi eet'weepathi-
aan, poog'weesi eem'sigithaaskeeyaan. Pag'wanta eet'weeyaan.
Just kidding. Maa-a taap'wee kinanaaskoomitinaawow,
kwayus soogi kinanaaskoomitinaawow. Igwa
kisageetinaawow. Oota oochi. Je vous aime, d'ici. I love you,
from here. Igosi n'tooteemuk. M'saw-awch keetawm
tapeepeek'skwaatag'wow...